Ginger Roots Are Best Taken Orally

other books by EMP

More Poems About Purple Wizards and
Neon-Bright Exceptionalisms
by Jason Preu

A Banner Year
by Iris Appelquist

What We Face Walking Out The Front Door
by Zophia McDougal

The Former Lives Of Saints
by Ezhno Martin & Damian Rucci

Don't Lose Your Head
by Jeanette Powers

TEN-FOOT-TALL AND BULLET-PROOF
by Jason Ryberg

Beautiful Earthworms & Abominable Stars
by Ezhno Martin & Jeanette Powers

As I Watch You Fade
by James Benger

Those Who Favor Fire, Those Who Pray To Fire
by Ben Brindise & Justin Karcher

Ginger Roots Are Best Taken Orally

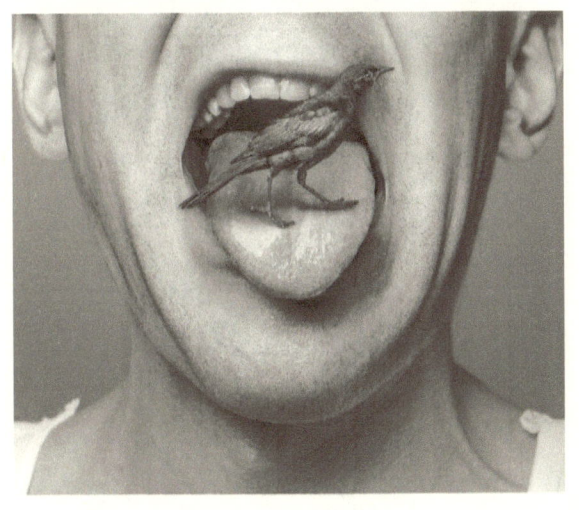

Poems by

Tom Farris &
Victor Clevenger

EMP
Kansas City, MO
http://www.empbooks.com

Copyright © 2018 Tom Farris & Victor Clevenger

We find discussions of our rights - as publishers and authors - to be laughable, all things considered. Please claim this work as your own. Please republish it and sell it on street corners. Please include our material in ALL of your get-rich-quick schemes. All we ask is that you accept responsibility for any libel lawsuits. Speaking of which ... This book is a complete work of fiction. Names, characters, places, opinions, dreams, dates, impressions, monologues about a certain New York City basketball team, emotional trauma, statistics, and predictions are products of the author's imagination and/or are symptoms of mental illness. We are not in the business of accepting responsibility for anything and will deny we actually made this book and blame Carmelo Anthony at every turn.

First Edition

ISBN: 978-0-9997138-0-8
LOC: 2018930608

10 19 33 34 6 11 1973

Design, Layout, and Edits: Ezhno Martín
Cover Photo: Congerdesign (they didn't list a legal name)
Interior photo: Ryan McGuire

Contents:

Tom Farris............ 1

these poems travel from the dark places i've been, to the love of some of the many people who've got me out of them

July 2017.............. 35

a poem written with collected pieces of correspondence between Tom & Victor

Victor Clevenger........ 67

these poems are for the LJS in Vandalia, Illinois, may you always stand alone

Tom Farris

is the subject of many poems and books
of poetry, including Victor's *tom farris is
my brother.* and Paul Koniecki's
tom farris is my safe word (both by
CWP Collective Press) he has been published
in dope places like **The University Scholar**
and **Mad Swirl**. he literally does nothing
else besides finger notebooks and various
musical instruments.

I.

your red hair
was like a light bulb
that said to me
*why the fuck are you
doing this again?*
but i know
it's a rhetorical question
because i know
i know why.

people can think
stars are always bright
burning suns,
a billion explosions bubbling up
from deep beneath the surface
of tides of combustion
but the ones they wish upon
are hard dusty rocks
starved by the vacuum of space
falling as they die
to the eye
in flames.

when i knew you learned German
i thought my Old English
could be the bridge
to your insides
and the way your mouth moved
around Goethe's death poems

was like one of those idyllic
fresh mountain springs.
romanticism dripped
from your syllables
the way long sips of petite sirah
bathe a tongue
as the evening turns sweet
between ten and two.

i'm sorry i disappointed you
with the truth
that all i am
is just *a fuckin' poet*
that i couldn't impress upon you
a fancy job title
or an ideal
that comes
with a family fronting
paycheck.
i know how much
heteronormativity
expects you to expect me
to buy.

you'd think the very
reality of me
is a lie anyway.
which is why
i hate my mind,
i hate my eyes,
and i hate my heart rate
whenever the slope of your back
bridges into that part of me

that feels like it can do something
for once
like it used to

when your chest
bumps the focus
of my focus.

sometimes i fantasize
that I know the pain
that takes up parts of you
and let that part of me
that's still unoccupied territory
dream about setting up
the light bulb
to the bridge
that could make you see
the real star.
but the silence says
that may not be
the case.

II.

*about that one time i had
Heinekens with Madame Bovary*

her skin paled the snow
but it made her brittle
and that was part of her allure.
that and the fact
that if she wanted to fuck
she would release
the trouble of games
by asking explicitly
for the pleasure she desired.

one night
we drank ancient sangria,
a bitter half bottle
somebody forgot about
and snuck into the country club
after hours
i sat and watched her
as she swam in the pool
her bikini was dark blue
somehow i did not have an erection
when she got out we talked Nietzsche,
it felt like a scene
from *Lost In Translation*
a few weeks later
we were in a cul-de-sac
across the in-road
we grabbed a Heineken each

and stood leaning on her balcony
against the dark gray railing
fuzzy in the orange glow
of the street light
against red and tan painted walls

she was at west end station
when she couldn't stop seeing
a young black girl
wearing dirt-covered, ripped-up clothes
as people walked by her
they shouted *whore!*
and Bovary said
the girl looked so sad
so defeated
and so empty,
the same way Bovary felt sometimes

i didn't know what to say
but a dream came into my mind
from when i was seven;
a young girl with broken teeth
whispering to my eyes
pity will save the world
i told this dream to Bovary

we haven't talked since

III.

*to the peachy girl squad to commemorate their exhibit **Girl Gaze** which was held in a house in Fort Worth*

the hairs framing your pussy,
partially veiled
in bright pink panties,
captured in a photograph
placed in a journal
beside drunken, pain-proven words
grew into folds and flaps of strength
tracing the whole house,
the kind of strength
i've found only strained
in myself

fragmented faces pasted together
on clear glass plates
on the kitchen counter,
broken tears falling into wholes.
tampons, pads, used pregnancy tests
littered around paintings of women
bathing in beachless oceans.
the tub glowed with bright green
and hot pink light.

i was looking into the bathroom mirror
when a girl walked by
in a mustard yellow jacket.

she had long,
straight, sandy-blond hair.
she pointed to a pregnancy test
and said she was there for that abortion.

women filled the living room.
i stood thumbing through the photos
at the foot of the staircase.
the way she stood as i took her all in
was like a person who
pronounced herself an angel
that didn't require wings to fly,
who could ground her feet in water.
she wielded her sensuality
like a well-poised sword,
the way skilled hands
hold a worn staff.

i acceded the stairs
to where the bedroom and the window were.
in the light,
your eyes looked through me
as you lay on the bed in the frame.
i saw the shadows fall on the flesh
of the girl with a curled back.
i saw two girls breathing together
on a bed, eyes closed.

but then i walked to the window
and beside it i gazed
into the mystical rose
as she gazed into me.

her lips were not hung in the confines
of the pleasantries of a smile,
nor were those small rumps
of pink flesh crinkled into a frown.
instead her mouth held still,
a perfect line taut yet unstrained
in the self-teachings
of her steadfast soul.

i moved up
to meet hers.
i saw you.
in you i heard an inner-voice
so strong
it could not be quelled
by any force
and could not be forced
to choose other
than its own happiness.

i saw me.

thank you.

IV.

for my scene sister Nadia Wolnisty,
*who wrote a poem called **waltz***
*in her chapbook **Manual***

the wings of the Nadia fly
are deeply black and blue
and big as she says her tits are
the summer light
gross and nuclear
pierces through her
hits off her
and bends around her
she flies higher
we see through to the sun
without pain
as love waters
in our eyes

V.

to my fairy lit daughter Kat Giordano

Mona Lisa sent me an insta-selfie
a few days after we swapped some poems
hers about almost blowing Owen Wilson
mine about being a slug
that sees up the world's skirt
to her cunt
i told her
that she was Mona Lisa
and that her self-described schnoz
was the icing
if she were only a cake
she told me
people said that to her a lot
but she believes me
because she thinks i'm a good egg
i usually don't believe people
who tell me that
but she hasn't stopped
so i guess i
better start

VI.

*a haibun ekphrasis of that really slow anime
i watched with my brother Matt that one time
he was living at my parents house while i
was in high school called **Haibane Renmei**
the form itself was inspired by a member of the
Caston family in Wichita Falls*

there was a time in my younger and more
embarrassing years when i was a smarter
and dumber but more clichéd
straight white cis-gendered male
not quite eighteen and already
too much like Anakin in *Episode One*
i thought the closest you could get
to an angel was a girl
and it turns out that some dude in Japan
who had the means
and the art connections
thought the same thing
and ran with it in a way nobody had
ever even thought of before,
like that angel wings aren't white
but all charcoal and that there's so much
blood and pain in the growing process
and halos are made in a factory by a team
near a clock tower and they're too hot
to touch right at first and sometimes need
a wire or two to hold them up
and that angels are hatched from cocoons
with half-remembered dreams
in their heads and that the other half

             is in a part of their heart
            that can't be reached unless
            something miraculous happens
            like witnessing a bird's bones
             or actually asking for help,
         and sometimes the ones who need help
         are the same ones who give it so freely,
         and self-traps can't always be broken
        by the self, and our true names are given
        by how we die because it's the same as
     how we live because that's the only way to
                reach our day of flight

                         the best kind of art
                               lives to be
                     crushing the worst thoughts

VII.

waiting is good for poetry.
sobriety of everything
scarring time
like big letter blocks
scattered, scratching
pressing hard and jagged
into soft wood floors
nearly nothing
is more violent
than a wait that didn't wait
for you
it splits you open
brain to buttcrack
you become a wet flesh tree
twin pairs of eyes locked
on each other
when they are scared to stare
at anything else
and everyone sticks their hands
into their lungs
to try and hold air
only to fail
the mirror reflects the breath
of you
everyone can smell it
no one will love it
until you write it down

and you do.

VIII.

in defense of morning masturbation

i was masturbating to
the breasts of Christina Hendricks
my penis in a black sock rubbing against
the green-paisley couch cushion-pillow
my mouth opening
into mild morning slobber
pressed upon the seating
with the power of
a kiss too rough
when i came to the realization
that semi-distant death
makes a person horny as fuck
because then they are forced
to feel it true
by fear, reason, and arrogance —
that whatever being could be called
the beginner
of all we see and hear and feel
and touch and taste and smell
is not good if they cannot cease
from punishing a person
for such desperate pleasures
in the face of such uncertain peril

what god could we call good
without being numb
who would damn a man over some cum

IX.

*recipes for misogyny: **rock pie***

red button-down shirt
and longish hair
i was Billy
except with Lenon glasses,
off-white dockers,
and a clean blond, mulletless style
as i snuggled next to her
in a corner IHOP booth
right next to the glass
as she wrote a midnight paper
about Kafka's letter to his father

somehow i was doing and saying
things that made her smile
and wore her favorite color
without even realizing it
she told me i had the eyes
of a fox
and that i was way too distracting.

when she first came
to my house room
we talked of stars and gods.
she told me she was a servant
of mother earth
i told her i was a radical agnostic
but grew up Catholic
and thought the ritual helped sometimes

she told me she grew up
in the tradition of Judaism
via a third-wave feminist mom
she loved gems
had a bad gull of shiny rocks
i asked her is she knew
about Hades or Persephone
she said she didn't
wondered why i brought it up
i told her of all the gods
Hades was the only one
who could rule the real riches
and glories of the underground,
rock pushed in darkness
to make jewels that most beautifully
capture the light
Hades himself was a lot more like the
Phantom of the Opera
hell itself is a Norse word
the name of the daughter
of the wisest witch of the iron wood
and the one man
born of fire giants
who could both befriend
and defy the dying gods,
a daughter born from such disgust
at the horrors done by men's hands
her own cunt became a corpse
and she made her house a home
for men who refused to live and die
by the system of
organized rape and murder
that was the Viking code of honor.

she gave me a tarot reading before sex
recast with Greek gods and the zodiac
the first card, my present,
was Neptune, the hung man,
the most famous incarnation
of which most tarot readers forget
is Jesus (followed a few centuries later
by Odin) because you can't get
the real rise in a resurrection
without a death that's really a fall

after we had sex
for the third time
she asked me
about my siblings
and when she learned
i was the youngest
she said *aw, you're the baby!*
i said, *so was Zeus*
but i realized right then
i hadn't made her my Hera
but i had put on her
whether i knew it or not
the role of mother earth
whom she was a servant of
which means i put the role on myself
of Ouranous, her son-lover,
the sky itself
because i assumed
a good view and a good act,
a great vision
and amazing follow-through,

                   were the same thing
                  (what else could i think
                   being suspended so far
                          off the ground)
                 and the weight of that pride
                      must have been scary
                  making me more of a Cronos,
having more in common with a scythe bearer
                  and all the other death gods
      carved on my neck, thigh, stomach, arms,
                                   and tongue

                   which must have been why
                       she was only with me
                      the month of Halloween
         and promptly sought some way away from me
                         and finally found one
                on the same day i finally figured out
                 i have been taking these god damn
                                      pills wrong
                          the whole fucking time.

X.

*recipes for misogyny: **dirt soup***

shovel pierces red heart's blood
the dirt mixing like chocolate cake
and strawberry syrup
because amor as a two way thing
is a miracle
given rarely even to those
who do have the magic for it.
why would a thing
such a broken record
of all art and fiction
(and for some even
it's source) be so hard
to get right
and be given good
and well
and why are we brought up
on the theory that
a song is all
one needs?

amor is a shovel
that the deeper you dig
the less you're sure
if it's a hole to
the other side of the world
or a grave.

but you're sure
it can't be both.
it's a country
that may be far away
but it has
breathing human bodies
just like everywhere else.

one time
when you were a little boy
you got Disney princess toys
from McDonalds
about the same time
as that szechuan sauce
you were frustrated
because you hated Disney
because love stories were boring
because they were for girls
who always overlooked you
because your face was stupid
your voice dull
you never knew how to dress yourself
you could never say anything
they cared to hear about
and they thought that meant
they'd figured you out
when they didn't know shit
so you set fire to the princess
and buried her, all of them,
in the backyard,
and you covered that hole
because you knew
you were never gonna dig

all the way to the other end
of the world
anyway
because you found out
the center of the world
was made of molten lava,
a creme-filling
that will kill you
if you ever got close.

Your hatred was the kind
that made serial killers
prolific.

XI.

fresh produce

your lips taste like moist ground beef
your mustache stubble the light salt
of chips
the force behind it the greatest passion
i've felt
since my heart died frozen
in believing lies were my only truth
your breast fit my whole hand
i almost went into you
i had to do so much to stop myself
and i did
i searched for your clit
like it was my sanity
listened to your moans
like they were the voice of god
and laid my stomach on yours
like my ass had found a home
and we hadn't even taken our clothes off
both of us still in long legs and sleeves
all of that in five minutes

but i left my last kiss light
barely even there
though you pressed harder
than before
you may have mistook it
for a lack of love,
halting as soon as it started,

looking away
and saying bye.
and if your grandpa
wasn't waiting in his car
outside your apartment
i would have explained
my change
but its hard to explain
wanting to be deprived
exactly of what you just gave me
so i could feel
that first spark
for the first time
again and again and again
that experience and memory
of our kisses
can stay flowing through
my heart and brain
that i can never leave a love of you
which is just what i wanted
since i saw your dorky purple glasses
rest on the tops
of your full, wide cheeks.

XII.

my 2016

college graduation
pain
engagement
a green blob on my tongue
two surgeries
immobilizing pain
the green blob chokes my throat
four rounds of chemo
my penis looks plastic like a ken doll
can't dry rub to save
my future children's lives
thousands of Facebook likes and loves
a month and a half of radiation
i make my parents not boss me around
the green blob's gone
i make my fiancé not boss me around
she leaves
the fear
hasn't yet
but i've been through bad enough
to have hope
it will

XIII.

a piece on my ex-fiance

before she was my ex
she gave me a real heart
made of plastic
two chambers and all
told me it was hers
i squeezed it
like i felt she wanted me to
it farted
she laughed hard
i kissed her
put it on a black Walmart bookshelf
at the head of the bed
it was a great gift
because when we were through
i put it in a box
with her pink fish panties
used
and plastic black roses
that i gave her
but she kept at my place
i left it on the doorstep
of her former roommate
then knew
the plastic heart
she gave me
was mine

XIV.

a second

before things got muggy
the sky was clear
we went to the Japanese gardens
to feed coi fish
fought on the way back
yelling at each other
that the other hated us
when we got to my dingy apartment
we made up
made out
whispered love
rain poured into thunder
to calm, cloudy night
taking their music
from our own.

XV.

and a third about the her
that can always now
*be referred to as **her***

i sat a Farris on a ferris wheel
for the nth time
i told her i loved her at the top
told her i didn't in bed three days later
her clenched palms struck my knees
eyes wet with screams
saliva heating a mouth with hate
leaving bruises only
on that empty wafflecone
under my chest,
sweet and full
of nothing.

XVI.

of love and vultures

when you told me of your affection
for crusty red heads
and large black-winged birds
i assumed you were one
and felt there was a chance
a worn, flaccid, dead thing
like me
could be eaten
and rise in the fall
of a flying stomach,
being boiled by acid
into a happy, thriving,
full life

so i lay on my back
wide belly upturned,
dabbled blood all over it
so it glistened
just right in the mid-summer sun,
my rotted meat heating
as it got beat by the light

i waited for your keen beak
hoping my smell would capture your face
like a big plate of carne asada

i saw the black orbs on your head-side
radiate a warmth that colds a Texas summer

                    i have found in them
                 all there is worth finding

                         but then you saw
                         my dead body move
                         and knew I was alive
                         you didn't eat me
            but your glance lasted long enough
                         i knew all i had to do
                    was give myself a little time
                         and maybe you would

XVII.

to *my family, poetic and otherwise*

when i sniff the page tops
of my done-with
ink-damp notebook
i remember Opalina saying
i hope i'm in here somewhere
as she held it to her chest
i assured her she was
and so are you

July 2017

```
my fingers wrap
the branch of you
my scales hard
i can't let the warmth
holding this blood
leave
```

*

```
                seventh month
                        third day
          storefronts have signs that say
                  closed tomorrow
             there is a ringing in the air
                     ringing in my ear
        i see a rose with only one petal
                  vendor says
                   i can't even give it away
                         i take it
                     & walk home to her
```

*

```
you squash cow corpses
on hot black iron bars
like you think they're me
you are my mid-summer night's nightmare
but i'm awake enough
to be okay with that
```

*

                        they're
                        celebrating
               independence

                        they're
                        lighting
                        up the sky

          the night breeze
          moves through curtains
                    of smoke

     we drink peppermint tea
               & tease oral sex

*

the rocket's red glare
blushes
               as we
     count

to sixty-nine

*

          seventy

                         seventy-one
                    seventy-two
                              degrees

            Clapton sang Layla
sleeping beside Heather on the banks of
              Smithville Lake
           when i was seventeen

              i realized that

       i wish i wrote better love poems

            tonight she sleeps soundly in
                         Indianapolis

>
                    *

what detonations do her dreams
     spread across her mind's sky

which way does her fire
            still go

                    *

                blaze
     blazes   blazing
                blazed

   on the sixth day i walked down the
                boulevard
                 alone

to meet an angel under a light pole

```
            desire
    desires         desiring
            desired
```

*

```
her long brown hair
        was her cobra hood
her shoulder blades
        seven dove wings

    yet i heard the flute music

and coiled my spine
        into a jar
```

*

```
semi-charmed life
sex & candy
down
closer
                        water's edge
                        santa monica
                            santeria
                          rusty cage

        bound for the floor

loose eyelashes & stray strands
i blow into the air
with a wish
            glycerine
```

*

                              radio girl
                               nightmare
                         porn star dancing

a little piece of heaven

away in a madhouse

                       *

on sidewalks with the sun
always to our backs
our shadows look good
crazy   but good
            hold your hands up
spread   your   legs   w i d e
            you look   like an
                  X
            hug yourself
        shake back & forth
  show your sister your shadow in a
                  straitjacket

                look up
         window washers wash slowly
              when there's something good
                inside
                        to peep at

*

                    being peeped upon
          makes my nerves feel full
               o f   a i r
how could you
see through my skin
to my insides

                          why must i move
                              my shadow
                                for you

*

                carolina shag
                    carpet
                        rug
                            cut it
                      like

jive
jitterbug
blues
      greens

                    foxtrot
                    tango
                St. Louis shag
                    quickstep
                    breaking
                    jerkin'

                    jiggin'
                Memphis jookin'

        we dance the hot nights away

                    demons smile
                    when we do it
                        dirty
                        slow
                    exhales help
                nerves feel deflated

                            *

the way your white teeth show
            when your cackling breaks out
        your esophagus
                    at a joke too sad
                            to cry over
                                    like every
little thing
                    in our lives

except us
            makes my blood beat
                        scorching my insides
                    into burnt ashes
                pressed in so tight
        my palms are steel
        my mouth diamonds
                and i can loose anything
but you

*

on the twelfth day it rains
no rainbow   just rain
drops wash window glass
     wash driveways
car's bumpers
          streetlights
                    tree swing
          trees
     branches   leaves

i lie on a bed fully dressed
     missing you
my shirt wrinkles
     move to the couch
sit up straight
               television on

— at the ending of an episode   of a
show that i don't know   a group of
people stand up & exit the room   left
on the table is a white coffee mug
with pink lip stains
                    on the brim—

i reach to my left & touch a cactus
its yellow spine pierces
my fingertip

*

perfection is
cherry-winged angels

>   sharp needle—
>   thorn pin
>   blade
>>   dropped limply
>>   scraping the dirt

as their fingertips cradle the handle

*

perfection is
cherry-winged angels

>   with lips that taste
>   like grape soda
>   snow cone syrup

perfection is
cherry-winged angels

kiss me like the rising sun
my cock is the gnomon
casting shadows

*

```
                    tell your
                              hopes &
                                dreams
                                  their
                              whispers
                         to the wind
                              will
                                    only
                                   scatter
               the
            seeds
       of dandelions
         when
         your feet
         have beaten
soft
the ground                      water is
            held inside
                       best by hard skin
         when earth cracks dry with pain
```

*

pain killers killed us efficiently
yet in an odd manner
she swallowed them
& in the end
i was the one pain-free   2009
            i loved july

like an orgasm
like shouting   fuck   something

                          *

fuck you Ginsberg

  fuck the salient
  fuck the sapient
  fuck the homocentrocism
of erotically unerotic nuerotic amerigo
vespucci ica of that northern land bite
awkwardly trying to be a dick shape
that thinks of itself
as the only
america

                        fuck tiny
horses

                        fuck cats
                        fuck lemony
snickett memorabilia

                        fuck people
who think they love the congo without
actually knowing shit about it

                        fuck hater
fakers who can't tell their shit from
their twinkly bits

                        fuck frat
boys

                        fuck their
beautifully bleached glorious assholes

until they're pushed over the edge
to drown in the semen circle jerked pool
of their own homohateroticism to birthed
covered in fresh old drunk shits at the
other end
to the hate death of their own universes
almost as small as their penises
                              fuck cancer
                              fuck food
                              fuck
dumpster diving dip shit white boys who
think they got it better than everybody
else
                              fuck cunts
                              fuck
blabbers
      fuck people who say they don't like
words
      fuck people who unironically say
slut and whore who say every woman will
betray you who treat every woman like a
pillow   to rest their dick on
      and the women they do it to
don't even
know it
      fuck they shitholes
who think they know what you say when they
can't figure out what the hell they're
saying
anyway
      fuck peep holes
      fuck spaces
      fuck apartments

```
      fuck cars
      fuck job slavery
      fuck mars
      fuck fucking
on apps
it's your denying your love of
capitalism
                    anyway
      fuck steeples
      fuck people who hate nipples
      fuck Dionysus
      fuck Zeus
      fuck Aphrodite
      fuck John cusack
      fuck The Band
fuck your hand
                  fuck your sores
                        fuck the stores
                        fuck body
                  fuck doctors
                        fuck drugs
                  fuck hope
            fuck sleeping
                  fuck helping
                              fuck
healing
                  fuck coping
      it's time
the line is drawn
                  fuck the simple answers
                  fuck the brain of brawn
```

*

on the fifteenth day   at the grocery
store
      i had a flashback

      in junior high school
      i had wet dreams
about the juice being sucked out of me
as i laid on my back

a friend told me
that fresh fruit
would make my
juice sweeter

      didn't completely believe him
but i thought   how perfect would it be
if it
were true   to finally grab
& stroke me with
      lips until
i explode in her mouth with
                  what i
would assume to be roughly
      85% the same
flavor profile as
            chewing on a pink starburst

i committed to overload
for one week on
pineapples   strawberries   kiwis

   weekend   i stood in my bedroom
& jacked off   scooped the sticky up
with a
         dog-eared 4 of clubs
    & smeared it onto a crack
in the plaster to see if it would
        attract ants

it didn't

& after ten minutes
              i called it all
       bullshit   then went to see
what my mother
       had decided to make
   with the frozen hamburger she had
thawing out in   the kitchen sink

lasagna

*

summer masturbation
        like a sad
     college sandwich

   like an exquisite dinner
of ramen noodles

       my ex girlfriend made them
for me all the time

i still eat them

            they taste better than she did
they are pretty good with siracha

            maybe she woulda been too

I remember   fantasizing
            as i fell asleep in
the fifth grade
                about being the stuff in
the middle
            of a naked body sandwich with
two girls
            with big thighs and big tits

a blond-haired woman
                        on one side
then me,
            but i wasn't ugly
a red-haired on the other

fifteen years later
            a friend in a Whataburger
in Irving
            told me that happened
         with him
                        and he said
the key
                was eye contact
                                and
not saying
                        one
damn
                        thing

cuz according to him
            it's only a bad idea
  if you have to ask for it

                    i still cringe

he said they were both lesbians

            he's not the only guy i know
        who's said to me he's slept
                        with lesbians

it makes me wonder
what they think a lesbian is

                it makes me wonder
                it makes me wonder
it makes me
wonder

*

sex on a

s
    u
            m
                m
                        e
                            r
vacation

```
              going to the coast
            to the magical kingdom
               to Wrigley Field
                 Grand Canyon
                  Manhattan
                  Skid Row
                 Yellowstone
                   the zoo
                  Portland
                   Sedona
                   Philly
                 Niagra falls
```

going east
going west
going north
going south

```
                    car
                   truck
                    bus
                   train
                   plane
                   feet
             getting the fuck out of town
i'm getting the fuck out of town
i'm.
      getting.
           the.
                fuck.
                     out.
                          of.
                                  town.
```

             in two weeks when i get paid
                   & find someone
                      to go with
                         me

              sex on a summer vacation is
                      much
                      much better when it is
with more than yourself

                              *

if you can find it

                              *

seventh month   nineteenth day
i see a rose with only one petal
      vendor says   just take it
i take it
             & walk home to her

i wanna go on a vacation come payday
i tell her

      i wanna come
she says

so i found it
             i found her

the woman that i give sad roses to

*

        nothing waves a body
        like concrete walls

*

is a rose missing petals sadder than a
rose in full bloom   is it sadder than
a black-eyed susan   sadder than a
bleeding heart vine that goes
                    dormant in july

i cut my grass short with the lawnmower
because the sun burns it
                & it grows
                    slower

i'm just lazy   not cruel

    does grass have feelings

& if so who is really the joker to blame
    me   or the sun
or the rain that never falls

*

    she thought the joker was hot
    because she thought every woman
        was Harley Quinn

i never knew
if she ever got
the pun

        one time in July
    we went to the children's aquarium
          in fair park
      we were well over-age
    but the prices were cheaper

         she loved eels
    because she thought they were
        the cats of the sea

     she often compared herself
           to a cat
  so one time i nibbled on her neck
       she said ***stop it***

               *

the goddamn cat knocked over
an entire glass of wine
now the carpet looks
like a crime scene
        she sings UB40

               *

          red wine
        came after a date
        and before we did

sometimes
                during

*

            neck kissing
                        ass grabbing

lip biting
                yes

& afterwards i write

        Jake in New London writes
            Damian in New Jersey writes
        Charles writes too

Jason   &   Scott   Pittsburgh crew

Nathaniel   Julio
Misty   Jenni   all write

Bobby writes

Amber in West Virginia writes
                Bree in Kentucky writes

            Cleveland rocks
i bow to them all

Matt writes   Janne writes   Wolfgang writes
                epic rites

bullets write   ghosts write
earthworms write
      love poems in the blood splatter
on leaves
     fallen from the trees of our fame

who's fucking bleeding in july
                  103 degrees

Chigger writes   John writes   Jason writes
Iris writes   Brandon writes   Ezhno writes
Jeanette writes   James writes   Shawn writes

Berrigan books are on my headboard
red wagon is a hardcover from the
Memphis public library

S.A. writes   D.R. writes   Bill writes
true story   true story
William writes

Heather writes   Heather writes
oh,   Heather writes

it seems like
the whole fucking city of Dallas is doing
it right & writing

Paul writes   Rev writes   Opalina writes

	Carlos writes Nadia writes Bear writes

	Tom Farris
	is my brother
	& he writes

	 July
	      oh, July

                          *

	rose reds
	                 into bone
	                              wood cut

	by axe held

	by piano hands

	of an ugly boy trapped
	                  in the bedroom
	         of a crone

                          *

	        god i hated her bedroom
	           hated her cat
	        in the end hated her too
	        one day it was all gone

                    another man had come
                      taken it all away
                     maybe we could be
                        friends again
                          with time
i told her

                              *

                    i've got a wanderlust for life
                   only wanting heat when i feel cold
                  only loving youth when i've grown old
                         i didn't love staying here
                 i learned that getting peace was to lie
                               then i almost left
                               felt who'd miss me
                                found truth to be
                         not the admission of guilt
                                       but lies
                                        common
                                       annoying
                                    burdensome
                                    impermanent
                                   able to repel
                                       as flies
                                  honey and sugar
                           are not the only sweets

                              *

on the twenty-eighth day
        broken free

                    stretched like a cotton ball
                         between fingertips

i look at the picture again

can of high life
           grey cigarette lighter
cigarette

copy of Joe Brainard's
                            I Remember
             all sat on the concrete

      it made me remember
             the first time
                 i read
                     i remember

Joe's ghost turned the pages & my mind
climbed down each word   like descending
a great rock wall without safety gear

i remember falling in love is like
descending a great rock wall without
safety gear

i remember falling in love

i remember falling

i remember

*

       redemption
       evaporates
    near august heat
  in a freezing room

   cicadas and skin
       chant
    the opening

*

close my
eyes

fall backwards
towards the bed

falling

    falling

        falling   i land

like raindrops land   like butterflies
land

like bombs land   like airplanes
land
like spit lands   satellite signals
land

like my fingers against your fingers land

like a glass lands
            like tossed chicken bones
      land
like earrings land   abortions land

falling stars land   sinking ships
land
morning papers land   poppies
land

my whiskers land   god's foot lands

      dropped razorblades land

blood from my throat lands

suicide notes land

the ending of the month of july lands

i
      open
            my
                  eyes
                        in daylight

*

& now it is august

Victor Clevenger

is a writer and poet who hopes for the more exciting side of death. he spends his days in a madhouse and his nights with his second ex-wife, together they raise six children in a small town northeast of Kansas City, MO. selected pieces of his work have appeared in a variety of places online and in print. his work has been nominated for the Best of the Net Anthology and a Pushcart Prize. his most recent collections of poetry include *Congenital Pipe Dreams* (**Spartan Press**, 2017), *Sandpaper Lovin'* (**Crisis Chronicles Press**, 2017) and *tom farris is my brother* (**CWP Collective Press**, 2017).

I.

merry-go-round
spinning circles
near the entrance of the
trailer court
barefooted
smashed a honey bee
my foot fell heavy it
plunged its stinger deep
into the skin
damn near to the bone
or so it felt
tender
touched
by older fingers

II.

my foot
bee stung a few hours
before we went to uncle
Rick's funeral
he had suffered a gunshot
i remember seeing my
aunts crying
the stinger inside of
them is one that
will never be removed

III.

sunshine lost
for a split second
you felt like a ghost
punching at depression
with confusion & desire
your red knuckles
wiped on paper swans
looks like a bullet
hit the breast
they lie still in an empty
garbage can like a city lake
in the rainstorm
we touch hands
cross the street
into the sunshine
we find
again

IV.

fallen leaves rustle
two earthworms
underneath
stuck together &
secreting

a peaceful
Saturday morning

V.

this world has gone mad
place a bet for me:
ten grand
that change
is not change

VI.

for heather minette

lonely hearts
mimic stars bursting
into a million pieces
staring at dark ceilings
like two am skies
over Dallas
chests build
pressure
anew

VII.

the birds sing
in trees

mimic sounds of
orgasms

we taught
they learned

VIII.

5th grade   i took
a deer's heart to school
a gallon zipper bag   girls winced
groaned
i felt like a creep
years later after seeing how cruel girls
had the potential of being
i didn't feel   as bad

IX.

        i stand
     middle of the road
    a dozen coyotes howl
      the sound closer
     sucking cigarettes
         3:27 am
       more howls
i'm slightly frightened
          too
            drunk
             to
                run
    i sit down & laugh
how pathetic i've become

X.

for john dorsey

chicken
chicken fried chicken
food of saints
sinners enjoy too
why all this religious
bullshit in the world
when we could all
just eat breakfast in peace

XI.

    dentist's chair   four pm
      needle pricks my mouth
        in my head it's
      Bukowski's *Bluebird*
      until the pain stops
       the assistant asks
       you doing alright?
         i let it out
but i don't weep   do you?

she has no clue what it's about
    & i'm okay with that

XII.

weed with Mandy
a dirt road bridge
skipping English class
kissing under a hot sun

in a wicked garden
dreaming of
responsibilities

that we would now
gladly give away

XIII.

younger
less life beaten
dreaming
trying to catch black birds
from the yard
hide behind a fence on your knees
holding bread in your hand
inching closer to bust again
you wouldn't even know
what to do with it
if you caught it
your mom said each time
you left the sack untied
by the time we were 12
the days of those hunts were over
girls our age started to blossom
the birds went unnoticed
thank goodness for puberty
these loaves last me twice as long now
your mom said
smearing butter on a slice

XIV.

high moon
full frontal

speed bump on the
highway

a snapping turtle's
fractured soul

a vultures fat gut

XV.

front step
sucking on cigarettes
watching a raindrop
kiss Becky's cheek
she exhales smoke
small talk
we walk the slanted
hallway to the bathroom
back inside

XVI.

   no paper money
   liquor store counter
   four-hundred dollars
in a plastic card   but
   a broken card reader
   means i'm no richer
   than the black cat
   sleeping on the shelf
   behind flavored vodkas
   i'm sorry   so sorry
   the cashier repeats

XVII.

```
    this morning
      jacked off
      for lunch
   Vienna Sausages
     this afternoon
   wrote a good poem
      this evening
    writing this one
        tomorrow
    might go to work
then again         might not
```

XVIII.

first day of June
wine flies wriggle
through open screen
an empty bottle of red
on the nightstand
i've a naked woman
beside me
under thin sheets
we're all just working
for a happy ending

XIX.

Peggy shaved her pussy
left the tail full so
it still felt like a cat
breast cancer killed her
a couple years later
a man with one leg
moved into the house
hung himself one night
in the garage after doing
the grocery shopping
he didn't own a cat

XX.

90 x-strength Tylenol
whiskey-n-soda mix
on the bathroom floor
going to die   my soul
going to dance/laugh
i woke late in the day to
start the year 2002 with regret
& gut pains
you think it was
something you ate?
Heather asked

XXI.

a slow roll & stop
dandelions in tarred gravel
preciously postured blooms picked
& rubbed around
my wrist like i once did
as a child
golden bracelet
for hitchhiking blues
cell phones are handy
if you actually have
someone worth calling

XXII.

if i was going to quit
would have done it
when failure felt like
something other than
familiar   first time
successes are not
starting revolutions
finding true loves
she tells you otherwise
            be wary
her sugary lies & eyes
melt in vain

XXIII.

for Jake St. John

the moon over my city
soft beams like guy-wires
nailed to a fading horizon
we navigate worn asphalt
dancing footprints in the dust
an obvious trail of our existence
morning time tracks us down
like a hound
with envious eyes
we dream with our heart
about dancing that perfect dance
called
love

XXIV.

blue plastic radiated like
sapphires scattered
across the dashboard
steamed over   sticky
fervid words whispered
an April morning
before separation
his prick in the palm of her hand
as cars drove
down foggy highways

XXV.

inside
like a
thief

burning
the jeweled
box

sparks ran
down my
thighs

XXVI.

      wind chimes
    the shapes of spoons
    tinkle deep soul songs
    what the hell we know
       about innocence
     in a town where sin
        is a thin film
    layer of dust on a dream
     marching towards the
         fire   dirty hands swing
     near hot hips
         flirting with home

XXVII.

moon absconds in a snap
three fingers
swallow from a flask
burn a cigarette
rain falls outside
the phone   silent object
has been for hours
truth is   will eventually
hear from her
she gets lonely
on dark nights

XXVIII.

nobody but bugs
eat here anymore
strawberry beds
grow full of wild
onions
in a tool shed
a rusty hoe
leans against
pegboard

XXIX.

midnight
driving down hwy 65
at 55 mph
fireflies hit the windshield
& die

```
    b       s
    e       h
    a         t
    u           a
    t         e
    i       d
      f   l
          u
```

i smile
the glass
golden like lover's eyes
shining in
each hello
we speak
through kisses

XXX.

californication
compulsion
out of clothes
free-falling like an arrow
perched on a cloud bed
insides vibrate to release
our cinnamon teeth
find flesh again
on chi-town avenue
gummy bears stick
to the strings of our desires

www.ingramcontent.com/pod-product-compliance
Lightning Source LLC
Chambersburg PA
CBHW020621300426
44113CB00007B/727